T0389817

DESERT

HABITATS

Written by
Alex Hall

Desert © 2024 BookLife Publishing
This edition is published by arrangement with BookLife Publishing

sales@northstareditions.com
888-417-0195

Library of Congress Control Number:
2025930397

ISBN
979-8-89359-318-1 (library bound)
979-8-89359-402-7 (paperback)
979-8-89359-375-4 (epub)
979-8-89359-348-8 (hosted ebook)

Printed in the United States of America
Mankato, MN
092025

Written by:
Alex Hall

Edited by:
Noah Leatherland

Designed by:
Jasmine Pointer

All facts, statistics, web addresses and URLs in this book were verified as valid and accurate at time of writing. No responsibility for any changes to external websites or references can be accepted by either the author or publisher.

Image Credits

All images are courtesy of Shutterstock.com. With thanks to Getty Images, Thinkstock Photo and iStockphoto.

Cover – Anait, Flash Vector, Maquiladora, SunshineVector, Volodymyr Voronov. Throughout – Tartila, Illerlok_xolms, Rocky Prakasit. 4–5 – Tetora Aihara, Teo Tarras, PANG WRP, James Nardelli. 6–7 – Mozgova, Abdulwahab Muhammad. 8–9 – Ward Poppe, hagit berkovich, Ken Griffiths, IgorMass, GreenSkyStudio. 10–11 – Gregory E. Clifford, Henry During, Alif Mauladani 17. 12–13 – Dennis W Donohue, Frank Fichtmueller, Maquiladora. 14–15 – Lubo Ivanko, Wolfgang Zwanzger. 16–17 – McGraw, Milan Zygmunt. 18–19 – McGraw, Shashidharswamy Hiremath. 20–21 – Deva Kaiser, Iammotos. 22–23 – Kenneth Keifer, Deliris.

CONTENTS

Page 4	Habitats Around the World
Page 6	Desert Climate
Page 8	Wildlife
Page 10	Desert Plants
Page 12	Greater Roadrunners
Page 14	Dromedary Camels
Page 16	Deathstalker Scorpions
Page 18	Life Cycles
Page 20	Protect the Deserts
Page 22	Our Desert Journey
Page 24	Glossary and Index

Words that look like <u>this</u> can be found in the glossary on page 24.

HABITATS AROUND THE WORLD

I'm an animal expert who explores habitats around the world. A habitat is the natural home where animals, plants, and other living things live. Are you ready to learn all about habitats?

Deserts are dry places. Dry habitats can be difficult for plants and animals to live in.

The Sahara

5

DESERT CLIMATE

Climate is the usual weather that happens in a place. In a desert, the ground and the air are dry. Most deserts are hot. But some are cold. Antarctica is the largest desert on Earth.

Sandy deserts are hot during the day.
However, they can get very cold at night.
The air and sand are too dry to stay warm.
So, heat is lost after the sun goes down.

It's time to explore different desert life around the world.

7

WILDLIFE

Deserts can be very hard to live in. Many living things have <u>adapted</u> to life in a desert habitat.

Meerkats have dark patches around their eyes to help them see in bright sunlight.

Fennec foxes have big ears that help them stay cool. The fox's ears can also hear <u>prey</u> moving underground.

Sidewinder snakes move sideways. They shuffle their bodies in an S shape to move quickly across the hot sand.

Can you move like a sidewinder snake?

9

DESERT PLANTS

Joshua trees are found only in the Mojave Desert. They have adapted to survive extreme heat. Some Joshua trees can even survive wildfires.

Joshua trees can live for hundreds of years!

10

Cacti have also adapted to live in harsh desert habitats. They grow spines instead of leaves. Cacti also have roots that go deep and wide. The roots can reach water far under the ground.

Wow! A greater roadrunner just ran by. Let's go find it.

GREATER ROADRUNNERS

Here it is! Greater roadrunners are birds. They live in the desert. To cool themselves down, they shake the fleshy part under their chin.

Many animals get rid of waste, such as salt, through poop and pee. However, this causes the animals' bodies to lose water. Instead, greater roadrunners release extra salt through holes near their eyes. This way, they don't have to get rid of salt through poop and pee. Their bodies can hold onto more water.

DROMEDARY CAMELS

Food and water are hard to find in the desert. When a dromedary camel eats, it keeps fat in its hump. The camel uses this fat for <u>energy</u> when it can't find food.

14

Animals have learned to adapt to life in a sandy desert. A dromedary camel has thick eyelashes that stop sand from getting in its eyes. The camel can also close its nostrils. This stops sand from getting into its nose.

Dromedary camels can walk long distances without getting tired.

DEATHSTALKER
SCORPIONS

The deathstalker scorpion is a deadly <u>predator</u>. These scorpions hunt mainly at night. They use their stingers to kill their prey with powerful <u>venom</u>.

Stinger

Don't get stung by these deadly critters!

16

Deathstalker scorpions can't always find food to eat. So, they can slow down how fast their bodies use food. This helps them survive on little amounts of food.

17

LIFE CYCLES

Life cycles are the different stages living things go through. One part of the cycle is to have offspring. The male and female deathstalker scorpion lock their pincers together before they mate. Then they perform a dance.

The female scorpion keeps her eggs inside her body. Then she gives birth to live young. They are called scorplings.

The mother scorpion carries her offspring on her back when they are young.

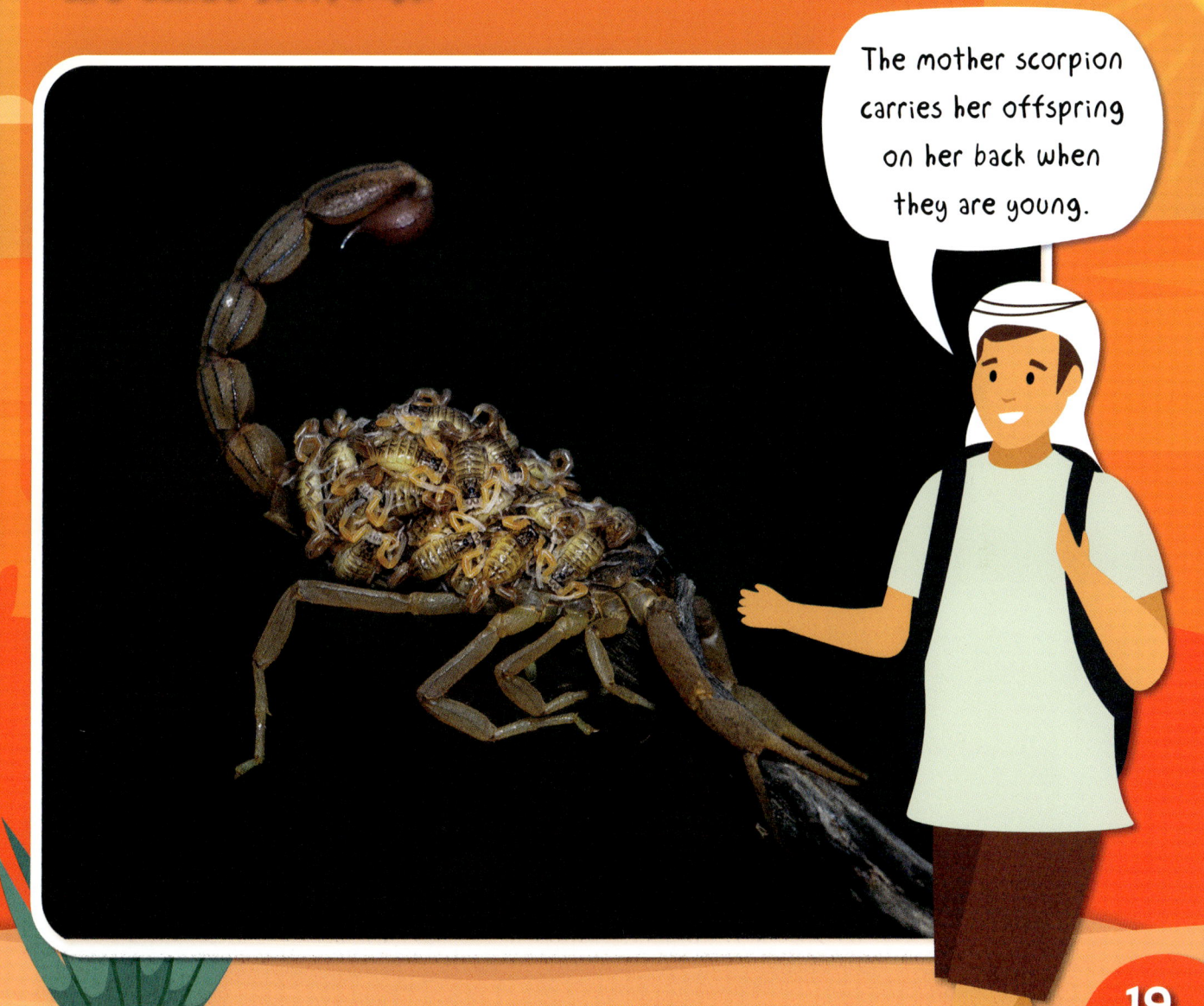

19

PROTECT THE DESERTS

Desert habitats are getting hotter. They are also getting drier. There is even less water for plants and animals. This is because of <u>climate change</u>.

People are working to slow down climate change. There are many things you can do to help! You can help <u>conserve</u> energy by turning off lights when you leave a room. You can also plant a tree. These steps can help slow down climate change.

What will you do today to help protect the deserts?

OUR DESERT JOURNEY

Phew! Exploring these scorching-hot habitats is heating up our knowledge of deserts. There is still much more to find out about these amazing places.

For life to continue in desert habitats, people need to slow down climate change. Maybe someday you will spot some more animals and plants on your own desert adventure!

23

GLOSSARY

adapted	changed over time to improve the chances of survival
climate change	crisis involving changes in the typical weather or temperature of a place
conserve	to keep from being wasted
energy	the power that makes living things able to move and live
predator	an animal that hunts other animals for food
prey	animals that are hunted by other animals for food
venom	a harmful substance that is injected through a bite or sting

INDEX

birds 12

humps 14

plants 4–5, 10–11, 20, 23

roots 11

sand 7, 9, 15

spines 11

stingers 16

sun 7–8

water 11, 13–14, 20